Don't Fall Out With the Cook!

WILBURN CARLOS

COMPILED BY

KIMBERLY F. CARLOS, Ed.D.

WILBURN CARLOS

ISBN: 0982213581
ISBN-13: 978-0982213582

WILBURN CARLOS

DEDICATION

To all fathers, grandfathers, stepfathers, brothers, uncles, cousins, and family friends who have championed music lessons, dance lessons, athletic events, bake sales, new outfits and a myriad of other things you might not be fully credited for doing, you have enriched lives like mine.

Thank you.

CONTENTS

FOREWORD

"Stay in good with the cooks
Forget how they may look
If you treat them kind and nice
They may feed you more than twice."

There were five things Daddy loved; music, God, food, his family and good looking women. Quite frankly, I wasn't always sure which came first.

Wilburn Carlos was nicknamed "Pee Wee" because he was smaller than many of his peers. This nickname traveled with him throughout life. People he hadn't seen in fifty years called him Pee Wee.

Daddy was even-keeled in trying circumstances. My mother said that once her car got stuck in the mud while they were dating. He didn't fuss or yell at her. She decided to marry him.

As a drummer, he once auditioned for Count Basie's band. He taught himself how to play the harmonica and the saxophone.

He had a distinctive whistle which could be heard from great distances. Daddy's appetite for life and its twists and turns could only be quenched by his transition into the next world.

This collection of Daddy's poems and short stories offers insights into his whimsical perspective on life. Please enjoy them, from his heart to yours.

ALL NUTS THEN

I threw some peanuts to the squirrels
And they were very mad;
They said, "These were the stalest peanuts,
We squirrels have ever had."

They said, "You take these peanuts back
Where ever you got them from,
And don't you mistreat us squirrels
Like we are some sort of bums."

"If your peanuts can't be fresh
Don't give us any at all.
Or we will call the Squirrels' Authorities,
And off to jail you will be hauled."

"They will punish you with great severity
Once they lock you up in jail;
And have you eating a ton of peanuts,
And each one will be stale."

"So the next time you give us some peanuts,
You right this down as a must;
You might wake up the next morning
And be eating stale peanuts with us."

FAINTLY I REMEMBER

In a yard I saw a baby's high chair,
And I remember when I once sat there.
Not in that particular one
But the one I sat in was lot of fun.

Around the table with the family,
Banging on my tray in front of me.
Spilling milk and food on the floor,
Baby screaming asking for more.

And when it is brought about,
It tasted nasty and I spit it out.
And there was my baby pen,
Turned upside down to keep me in.

I felt like a prisoner in a cage,
I would yell out and go into a rage.
Now the chair sits empty and alone,
As a reminder sits in our home.

When I was a child and there I sat,
With pleasant memories I can't forget.
Now that I'm grown with worries and cares,
Sometimes I wish to return to my little high chair.

A SLIMY, SLIMY FRIEND

The cold snake lay on the ground
Not a movement or a sound
As he breathed his last breath
Not too much of his life was left

A kind man happen to come that way
Saw the poor snake lying there
"Let me take you home," he said
And get you out of this air.

He laid the snake down by the fire
And gave him food of his desire
As the snake seemed to get well
He was very happy you could tell.

As he crawled around on the floor
He would stop and crawl some more
He crawled by the man in the chair
And looked at him with a stare.

Slowly, without haste
He wrapped himself around his waist
"What are you doing to me my friend?"
Said the snake, "Your life must end."

As the snake began to squeeze
The man hollered, "Stop, stop, stop, please."
"You are crushing me to death;
Stop, I am running out of breath."

"Why are you doing this to me?"
"I took you in as a friend;
Now my life to you it seems
You want to end."

My motto as a snake
Never give your prey a break
The next time you are headed home
And see a dying snake, leave him alone.

A LONG SHORT STORY

To make a long story short, some speakers say
It seems to take them forever and a day.
When you think they're about to end
Their introduction has just begin.

DOGGONE IT

He chased two rabbits, but they were smart;
They ran together, then ran apart.
The dog stopped and scratched his head,
Didn't know which way they fled.

There was a tree, he sniffed the trunk;
He was surprised when out came a skunk.
He decided quickly to run away,
And chase the rabbits another day.

WILBURN CARLOS

I AM HERE FOR YOU

Fathers who believe in their daughters
Give them the courage to succeed;
Through prayers and supplication
And whatever else they may need.

YOU HAVE NOT LEARNED YET?

To rely on others is to be disappointed
This you will soon learn and find
You may wonder why so many people
Are carrying a confused and trouble mind.

But you said, "Oh, I forgot,
Something else came up very hot."
"I had other business to attend,
I had to go and meet a friend."

If you really want something done
Make yourself a committee of one
Get up and do it yourself
And please don't rely on someone else.

MY MUTT THE HERO

A stray dog I took in,
Soon we became the best of friends.
He wagged his tail when he would eat,
And at night, he rested by my feet

People would call him a mutt,
And asked, "Where did you get that such and such?"
We became buddies so much so,
He would follow me wherever I would go.

As we walked down the streets,
The neighbors we would meet.
They would poke fun at both of us,
But we never had a quarrel or fuss.

One night when all were sleep,
My little dog let out a beep.
As he began to bark out loud,
He smelled smoke from a spark.

As I awoke from my bed,
Smoke was spreading over my head.
His bark was so strong and loud,
He woke up the sleeping crowd.

The people jumped from under their sheets,
And headed out towards the streets.
They all escaped safe and sound,
Because my dog was lying around.

Call him a mutt, whatever you like,
He was a hero for that night.
I saw a mutt and took him in,
And the mutt and I became good friends.

GO TO THE BACK OF THE BUS

They told me to go to the back of the bus
I went back without a fuss.

As I walked towards my seat
Suddenly, I heard a very loud squeak.

All that sat in front of the bus
In the accident they were crushed

When they now say, "Back of the bus,"
I go back without a fuss.

I'm alive, I survived.
And if they knew "go to the back of the bus"
They also would have come too.

WE TRIED TO MAKE THE LIGHT

We left the party rather early
To make it home before night
Suddenly, there was a terrible crash
Because we wanted to make the light.

Injuries, broken bones
One even lost their sight
It never would have happened
If we hadn't tried to make the light.

Cautions, warnings, many they gave
If we had listened, perhaps a life would have been
saved.

No, we were driving with all of our might; trying
very hard to make the light.

Now darkness fills many families' rooms
With sorrow and much gloom.
It never would have happened
Had we been driving right,

But we wanted to prove to ourselves
We could easily make the light.

PEE WEE THE SHOE SHINE KING

Many other things people could do
Pee Wee learned how to shine a shoe.
He learned from a fellow named Tommie Lee, who
soon became his best hommie.

Tommie could make a show rag pop
Louder and faster than a jackrabbit could hop.
If you could pop a rag in those days
A tip was surely to come your way.

A whisk broom was always a must
To brush off lint and other stuff.
When you would finish brushing the man, you
came around with an open hand.

Into your hands he would drop
A small tip which then was a lot.
Shoes were ten, fifteen and twenty cents a shine
Pee wee said, "I can get more for mine."

A printed sign read over his head
"Asking for 25 cents, or a quarter instead."
Something you got you didn't expect
An outside parlor with a free rain check.

There were times when it would rain
People came to Pee Wee just the same.
Whenever a shined shoe left his stand
Folks would ask, "Where did you get that man?"

Pee Wee's shines were so discreet
Some would last longer than a week.

Then other shiners began to say,
"I'm gonna raise my price today.
The quarter shine became the thing
Because of Pee Wee the shoe shine king.

RING DING

On her finger was her wedding ring,
Which didn't account for anything.
Often she would go away but couldn't stay, because
her loved one was coming home the very next day.

The couple would check in an exotic place, where
no one would recognize their strange face.
There they were laughing, drinking, having a ball,
when suddenly she spotted someone across the
hall.

The one she loved was standing there,
And at each other they just stood and glared.
"What are you doing here," he replied?
She seemed nervous, fidgeted, and try to lie.

"They told me you would be stopping in here, so I
came to meet you my dear."
"This is Roger, the teacher at Danny's School."
"He's teaching him behavior and other such rules."

"Come Darling, let's all have a seat,
Roger, this is my husband I'd like for you to meet."
The waiter came wearing a happy smile, saying,
"Hello lovebirds haven't seen you in a while."

"You are the Brother from the army I was told,
looking at those medals; Bronze, Silver, and Gold.
"Melissa what's been going on since I've been
away? Why did the waiter call you Evelyn and your
friend Jay?"
"Those rings on your finger don't mean a thing,
while I'm fighting a war, you have yourself a fling.
I'm going to leave and let you lovebirds be, and you
won't ever have to worry about me."

"I'm going to go and pick up my son
While you lovebirds have yourself some fun."
"I was somewhat suspicious all the time, now I can
rest, and have peace of mind."

Rings now in window, both for sale,
Life was once happy; later grew stale.
Two lovely rings now on display,

Husband, Wife, and Roger have gone their
separate way.

P.S. To some wearing a ring, it doesn't mean a
thing.

GREED AND GREEDY

The appetites of greed and greedy
Takes more than they actually need
And never seems to get enough.

Though they may be bursting at the seams
Their greed they will continue to stuff.

HOW ABOUT A TASTE?

Standing on the corners
Hustling up a drink.
Which will only affect the mind,
So that it cannot think.

The heart, kidneys, ribs and bladder,
Being destroyed doesn't seem to matter.
When the damage is over and done,
Will you look back and wonder where was the fun?

Now going through life with aches and pain; can
barely walk now leaning on a cane.
No longer on the corners seeking a taste,
Health is now gone; consumed, what a waste.

I WANT A SUGAR DADDY

I want a Sugar Daddy
And don't care how old he may be.
As long as he's got enough sugar
To satisfy little old me.

I'd gotten myself up a financial tree
And I need a Sugar Daddy to come and rescue me.
It doesn't matter what the folk may say
Sugar Daddy can come to my house and stay all day.

His sugar can be brown or even white,
But green sugar will set things right.
I'm deep in debt as I can be,
And if you know of a Sugar Daddy
Please send him to me.

ACCESS TO DEATH

She was a constant smoker in her store,
And cigarettes were what she adored.
She would reach over with her hands,
And pick out her favorite brands.

She never paid it any attention
Or cared to know.
Inside her body was decaying slow.
She would light up and take a puff,
Never knew when she had enough.

Many smokers will do the same,
Not knowing it's ruining their health and brain.

Access to death they are unaware,
I don't think some really care.

Some things that are access free,
It's better sometimes to let them be.

ONE HUNGRY LEOPARD

One hungry leopard lying in the tree
Looking to eat what he would see
He saw an elephant it was to big
He rather settle for a deer or pig.

Crawling by was a huge snake
He didn't want to be bother with a tummy ache
Then he spotted a grizzly bear
Lots of meat but too much hair.

Then the leopard dozed off to sleep
Dreamed he had plenty to eat
Fried chicken and turkey legs
Bean soup and a pan of bread.

A half of cow and half of mutton
His eating burst his belly buttons
He drank and drank until he burped
Suddenly! He fell and hit the dirt.

He got up from the ground
Food nowhere to be found
One hungry leopard by the tree
A wonderful, wonderful dream had he.

THE BLACK WIDOW

The Black Widow she was named
Killing to her was just a game
After an affair she was satisfied
Later on her lovers would die.

Many sought to gain her love
Only to learn there was none of
She was overwhelmed with beauty and glamour
But in her heart were terrible manners.

Those she was able to capture their eyes
Soon vanished like a cloud in the sky,
There may also come a day
When you too may be led astray.

The advice one can give or say
Be careful, lest you go that way
I let the Black Widow sit and wait
To offer hiding death inside my gates.

LADY, I DID NOT KNOW!

Lady, I'm having your husband's baby,
He came into the club one night.
Telling the folks he was Mister Right.

He went ahead and ordered some drinks, and he
was dressed down wearing his pink.

Out of his pockets he pulled out a roll,
Of green bills he began to unfold.

He came up smiling in front my face,
And said, "Let's you and I leave this place."

I grabbed my jacket and my purse,
He opened the door and said, "Ladies first."

He was charming and very polite,
And together we had a good time that night.

He said, he once was married his wife passed away,
and loneliness keeps him company every day.

He pulled out a box and inside was a ring; He
hoped to find someone who will do the right thing.

I was happy as I could be; at last I found someone I
loved, and someone loved me.

Much time together we spent at my place; he would
bring pretty flowers to put in my vase.

And sometimes he would bring expensive perfume,
and the lovely aroma would saturate the room.

After seeing each other for quite a while,
I told him I was pregnant, carrying his child.

One day we were walking down the streets, and old
friend of his we happen to meet.

Her face was radiant with smiles and joy, and said,
"How's the wife, the girl, and the boy"?

I stood there speechless couldn't say a word;
I couldn't believe what I had just heard.

After she had left I looked him in the eye, and said,
"Is she telling truth, or is it a lie?"

"What you did to me I don't think it was nice.
Take me to your home to meet your wife."

"Lady it's hard for me to say,
But your husband has led me astray."

"I am pregnant carrying his child,"
She looked at me with a pitiful smile.

She said, "My husband is much more younger than
I; He is not truthful, but full of lies."

"He dresses nice and talks real good,
He's got the women fooled in the neighborhood."

"I clothe him, feed him, and give him money each
day; I don't want him to leave me and walk away."

"I asked him to marry me for many years; to be tied
down is something he fears."

"You are not the only one that came to my door;
there has been a dozen or more."

"He sleeps all day and runs all night,
Frankly speaking, he is not the marrying type."

"I know my man and I know him well,
Every woman he meets, he's got a story to tell."

"Sometimes I see him, sometimes I don't;
He's like a child; doesn't know what he wants."

"He is like a rolling stone, he can't be still; all he
wants is a good time and a thrill."

"So honey, do for yourself the best you can; no
matter what happens, he will always be my man."

MRS. PARNELL'S SON JIMMY

Jimmy was his mother's son
In fact, he was the only one
He was tall, handsome, and sort of trim
To his mother, there was none like him.

Once Jimmy was engaged to a beautiful girl; when
the army called him to see the world.
Shortly married, he left his job and wife
And in the army, he started a new life.

He slept on bunks, even on the grounds
As he traveled from town to towns.
Something strange happened to Jimmy
One night, it was described as a terrible sight.

Something bit him as the story goes
Just what, no one knows.
He didn't seem to suffer any pain

But Jimmy that night was never the same.

It affected his body and his mind
That the army pulled him out of the line.
He was taken to the hospital tent
And for Jimmy a doctor was sent.

They examined him from head to toe
His condition was so bad; they had to let him go.
He was discharged and sent back home
Soon he found himself lonely, and all alone.

He returned to his job, they pushed him aside
His sweet wife left him, to no longer abide.
To see Jimmy then, you would be amazed
He now walks around in a daze.

His loving mother, stood by his side
Up until the day he died.
As she suffered his pain and grief
Death came and brought him relief.

I met Jimmy; he was nice as he could be
To his mother, there was none liked he.
Mrs. Parnell had a son
Jimmy was his name, the only one.

LEAST EXPECTED

Rain, rain please go away
Please come back another day
So we may go out to play.

Now that the old rain is gone
We can go play all day long
Let us pack ourselves a lunch
And go to the park where we can munch.

Off to the park let us go to hop, skip, run to and
fro.
See how bright the sun does shine; we are going to
have a wonderful time.
I see a cloud forming in the sky
It's gonna pour water on you and I.

"To you must I explain?"
"Remember me, I am the rain."
"You're the one who told me to go away, and come
back some other day." "Today, I have chosen this
spot; and I'm here to stay, like it or not."

"The next time you tell me to go away, go into the
house if you want to play." "And let me rain if I
may, if I chose a bright, sunny day."

WAKE AND WRITE

When I lay down in my bed
And sleep through the night
A voice speaks to me saying,
"Get up, get some paper and write."

And sure enough comes wonderful stuff.
If I should hesitate or delay
The very next morning those thoughts will go away.

JUNGLE LUCK

As the Jaguar walked the jungle ground
Slowly, quietly without a sound
Crouching low looking for prey
To be his meal just for that day.

Suddenly, in his sight there appeared
A lost mother's baby deer.
As the deer moved slowly along
When the Jaguar gets him, he will be gone.

What the Jaguar had failed to see
Was a small monkey up in the tree.
As the little creature by the Jaguar came near, the
monkey was watching with trembling and fear.

Quickly, the monkey let out an EEK!
The baby deer ran, left behind a streak.
The Jaguar looked up at the monkey and said,
"If it had not been for you, I could've been fed."

APRON STRINGS

Mothers, let go of your apron strings,
And let your children go out to play.
If you taught them all correctly,
I'm sure they won't run away.

Let them travel and explore,
Don't keep them inside behind closed doors.
Let them meet people and have some friends;
For you to let go, it won't be your end.

They each must grow up sometimes,
And train them while they are at home.
And when the apron strings are cut,
They'll know how to act on their own.

TOO UGLY TO BE SEEN

Ugly girls were only dated at night,
To be seen in the day time was a terrible sight.
To keep from being embarrassed of what might be
said, you would put a sack or a bag over her head.

The folks would never know what was under the
bag; it could be a witch or a runaway hag.
Her ugliness was hid inside, to protect your self-
esteem and your pride.

HELP FOR HONEST JOHN

I saw a book on how to steal without getting caught
I'd saved up my money, and that book I bought.
I looked up the author, to no avail
For some reason he was back in jail.

When I visited him he was at his desk
"What are you writing John?"
He answered, "How to get out of this mess."

NEVER A MISS

When Nana came to the stove to cook,
We would gather around just to look.
She would make a large pancake batter,
If some spilled on the table, it really didn't matter.

When she took out the large skillet or pan, we all
had to sit, none could stand.
She didn't want us to be near the fire,
Because an accident one just might acquire.

Now for the exciting time to come around, she
would flip the pancake in the pan upside down.
She was very, very good at this,
And at no time did she ever miss.

AIRBORNE

As he went searching on the ground
Seeking food if some could be found.
Not too far above his head,
Was a terrible Hawk, whom all the squirrels dread.

Suddenly, the poor squirrel was snatched; now he is
today's catch.
As he was being carried into the air,
On his face was fear and despair.

Soon the Hawk flew back alone
He had found food that day for his home.
Now whenever a Hawk is near, the wise squirrels
will quickly disappear.

HAS IT REALLY BEEN THAT LONG?

I heard the young people call me pops
Some even call me dad
I remember not long ago
I was merely just a lad.

Shooting marbles, flying a kite
Having fun both day and night
My youth I had is now gone
Tell me, has it really been that long?

I was single not long ago
I now have children, more than four
My youthful days were well spent
As I look back, I saw where they went.
Time has caught up with me now
My expectations are yet very strong
I have now reached that golden age
Tell me, has it really been that long?

NURSING HOME CANDY MAN

I may be sleep when you come
Or I may be just away
Please leave my candy on the stand
And I'll know you've been here today.

LADY MAGNOLIA

Lilac eyes and crimson lips
Fresh as the morning mist
Magnolia charms with open arms
Waiting to be kissed.

WORDS FROM THE BIRDS

We flew down to get a meal
And there was a scarecrow in the field
He was lumpy, full of straw
The saddest scarecrow we ever saw.

As we flew through the air, we wanted to see why
he was there.
We heard the farmer shout the other day; "I must
do something to keep the birds away."

Well, we lit on the scarecrow's arms
And from him we felt no harm.
So we said, "He's not real; Let us go and get a
meal."

Well, we got some corn and wheat
And whatever else we wanted to eat.
Then old farmer brought out his gun
With no intention to have some fun

Suddenly there was a bang bang sound
So we hid ourselves quickly on the ground.
If we had taken to the air

Our lives he wouldn't had spared.
So we lay amongst the berries and grapes;
Chuckled while we laughed and ate.
And the lumpy scarecrow stood by
Watching with his strawy eyes.

He said, "The danger is now gone
And you birds better get along
So whenever you want a meal
Stop anytime now; you know I'm not real."

MY EMPTY CANDY BOWL

My candy bowl now sits alone,
Full of candy once in my home.
Whenever the family or the kids would come,
From the bowl they would take some.

I saw to it that it was always full,
Even when they headed off to school.
Some they carried off in their bags for lunch
Not a few pieces, but a bunch.

Now that all of them are all grown,
The candy bowl now sits alone.
I always kept the kind they liked,
Sometimes over the pieces they would fight.

I look at the bowl now with great memories,
How exciting and joyful it used to be.
Once upon a time the candy bowl held plenty,
Now all is gone as it sits alone and empty.

EGGS ON THE WALLS

We would take our mother's eggs
From the old ice box
And thrown them against the walls.
When time came to eat breakfast,
We had no eggs at all.

To us it was a lot of fun
Throwing eggs and watching them splatter.
No eggs in the morning for breakfast,
For us it didn't matter.

We had plenty of bacon on the table
And gravy and biscuits too.
When time came to bring out the eggs,
There were only just a few.

"What happened to my eggs? said Mother;
"They were right here alongside the butter."
"These kids of mine sure eats food fast,
No wonder food around here doesn't seem to last."

I came home the other day
And I was amazed and really appalled
To see that someone had splattered
Some eggs against those walls.

Kids will be kids so they say; I am so glad my kids
will never throw our eggs away.

"Shh! Hush up! Don't tell Mom."

WE WERE HERE FIRST

A piece of bread lay on the ground,
The sparrow, the black bird by each was found.
A bushy tail squirrel came out of the tree,
Said, "This bread is just enough for me."

So the sparrow and the blackbird each stood back,
And watched the squirrel nibble while his lips
smacked.
"That's not fair," said the birds to the squirrel,
"You must think you own this entire world."

"Besides, we were here ahead of you,"
Said the squirrel, "That don't mean a thing.
Even though you were here first,
I'm the biggest, so that makes me king."

GATOR ACHE

Had he knew
He wouldn't had bitten off
More than he could chew.

The alligator was swallowed by the snake
His tail gave him a stomach ache.

If he had only known,
He would have left that alligator alone.

The poor snake turned black and blue,
For biting off more than he could chew.

THEY WILL GO ON WITHOUT YOU

He took his ball and bat and went away
No ball games were played that day.
Because he took his ball and bat and went away.

He hit the ball and it was caught,
He was angry and back he fought.
He took his ball and bat and went away
No ball games were played that day.

He brought his ball and bat for us the next day
For us to have fun and also play.
He was put out running to second base,
The way he acted was a disgrace.

So he took his ball and bat and went away
No ball game was played that day.
Someone else had a ball and bat
We played afterwards; there were no spats.

He sat down one day with his ball and bat
And watched us play hit and catch.
If you think you're the king on a throne,
You may find yourself sitting all alone.

Somewhere someone will let you know,
People can do without you and will let you go.

THANKS FOR WHAT?

I did not say thank you
And the reason why
What you gave me
Wasn't enough to feed a fly.

We may stare and look appalled
After giving our best and our all.
Oh how quickly we forget
When our needs our swiftly met.

Later on we may regret
Allowing ourselves to get in debt.
While trying to help out a friend
And later come to a bitter end.

SOME PEOPLE

Some people have the mind of a thief,
Some people have the tongue of a liar.
For some people to do the right thing,
Is not some people's desire.

THIEVES' SEASON

Thieves do not live around here,
At time they do come through.
And they will steal anything of yours
Whether it's old, small, or new.

Police signs read, "Beware take heed,"
Thieves nowadays can hardly read.
They will take your valuable stuff,
And sell them for just enough.

For a habit they must feed,
Money they must have
Money they desperately need.

So protect your property and put it away
So the thieves won't steal from you one day.

IT USED TO BE

There's no place like home
Years ago they would say,
But where there is quarreling
And tempers are boiling
It's best to go away.

SUDDENLY SHE DISAPPEARED

For her it was love at first sight,
She had money problems and was uptight.
Quickly she got herself engaged,
It did not matter concerning his age.

He was much, much, older than she,
And he was now her husband to be.
They got married and had their honey moon;
afterward trouble started for her real soon.

Word quickly to the family soon got around,
A new gold digger just hit town.
She now got papa, my Uncle Fred,
And waiting to get his money when he is dead.

The family got together with their scheme,
To destroy papa's wife and her dream.
Papa's new wife he loved very much,
While she worked on him her golden touch.

The family members got her to go with them, as
one big happy family saying we all are friends.
The precious little angel showed no fear,
That night Papa's sweet wife suddenly disappeared.

Papa began to wonder where his wife could be,
"Why can't she pick up the phone and call me?"
The family members went by his home,
Saw he was worried and felt alone.

Each one to Papa began to say,
"She probably went shopping for you today."
"Go on to bed, get your rest;
She's making sure she gets you the best."

Well the little angel never did return,
And Papa's heart for her really did yearn.
Now the money in the family all will stay, and will
be divided up when Papa passes away.

MY DIARY

A diary is sort of a special book
No else is supposed to peek or look.
It is private, precious, and personalized
And tells of events, people, and also guys.

In my diary it also contains closest friends and
special names.
Sometimes I'm not feeling at my best
I'll take out my diary from my desk.

In it I began to ponder and write
Things that happened to me that morning or night.
In my book I am able to confide
To write my thoughts that comes to my mind.

My Diary is truly my best friend, and our
conversations never seem to end.
I feel happy, joyful, and care free
As my diary remains silent and listens to me.

It never gets angry or goes into a rage
When I begin to write upon its page.
It stays calm and gives me a thrill and tells me to
write down whatever I will.

LIFE WILL GO ON

Once he came home early and found her in the
arms of another man, so he went and took the gun
off the shelf, and went upstairs and shot himself.

Whether a person chooses right or wrong
No matter what happens, life still goes on.
People have in their minds what they want to do,
To be dishonest, unfaithful, deceptive or true.

Trying to satisfy yourself may be hard to do
Remember life will go on, with or without you.

BOTH ENDS AGAINST THE MIDDLE

She kissed one in Chicago the other in Detroit
They each not knowing they were being exploit.
Each one knew nothing about the other
She was playing both sides underneath the cover.

None gave the other a thought
As long as they were getting what they ought.
Playing from the middle can be a dangerous game
It can cause embarrassment or get you maimed.

WHAT A BITE THAT NIGHT

Thieves kept breaking into his store,
And he would get angry and sometimes sore.
He told the authorities and they said,
"Stay up all night and don't go to bed."

They said it to him as a matter of fun,
But he knew himself this couldn't be done.
So he went out and caught him a rattlesnake,
And put him in the store for safety's sake.

Well, the thief that night was greatly surprised
When he saw that snake before his eyes.
Suddenly he began to tremble and shake
For the thief that night, there was no escape.

On the hand the thief was bit; on that night his
stealing quit. No more break-ins in that store
The rattler put a stop to them forever more.

What a bite that night.

CHECK FIRST BEFORE YOU FLIRT

If a woman says take her shopping for some clothes
And starts pointing saying, "I want some of those;

Buy me some dresses and pocket books
And several coats to put on my closet hooks."

You'd better check your bankbook and your wallet,
And be sure your credit is solid.
If you both should be walking down the streets,
And the finance company you should meet;

If your payments have not been paid,
You just may end up on the sidewalk dead.

You gave her the impression you were well off;
You own your own company and you were the
boss.

Little did she have the slightest thought;
You couldn't afford the things you bought.

If there is talk of a honeymoon; you'd better
postpone that date real soon. If your debts you
cannot pay, start planning for a quick getaway.

TRUST

Oh! How happy we can be
If I can trust you and you can trust me
Together we are one
Together having so much fun.

Together we shall ever be
Because I trust you, and you trust me.
No worries or any fears
Our trust for each other is precious and dear.
Happy together we will always be
Because I trust you and you trust me.

UNFAMILIAR FACES

Once when I walked down the streets,
Many faces I knew I would meet.
No matter where if in strange places,
I still would see many known faces.

Now it seems no matter where I may go,
I see many face none that I might know.
As I move about now and then,
Seldom do I meet a face of a friend.

I now look, stare and what do I see?
Stranger faces looking back at me.

Now they all seem to have disappeared,
Though I was close, to them I was near.

Where have the faces gone I once knew?
The ones I see now are different and new.
These things happened in a period of time; soon
they will be asking what happen to mine?

YOU MUST BE TWENTY-ONE

You must be twenty-one my son
Before you have to learn
That the whiskey in these bottles
Is strong and most likely to burn

Several more years my little man
And perhaps you will see
That these places you so desire
Are not the places for thee.

RETURN TO YOUR HOME

Spider, spider, on my walls
If I crush you, that will be all
This time I will let you go
You may have a family; I don't know

Your children will ask, "Where is Dad?"
"Mom, what I say, may sound sad
He was in a house on a wall
He was crushed badly in a hall."

But the man in the house
Knew he had children and a spouse
So he let Dad stay and crawl
On his ceiling and his walls.

THE GROUND HOG

In cold climates it is said
If the groundhog sees its shadow
There will be cold weather up ahead.

But when the weather is always warm
And the sun doesn't all the time shine
The groundhogs you will not find.

So if the weather on us depends
On what the groundhog may see
Keep him down in his hole
And let those groundhogs be.

I DO REMEMBER SNOWBALLS

I was driving my car down the streets one-day
When a flying snowball came my way.
I glanced up with a smirky looking smile
And saw it was coming from a very small child.

I remembered back then in my time
When throwing snowballs was always in line.
We found snowball throwing a lot of fun
Especially if you hit your target, broke and run.

When we saw kids riding on a sled
We would throw snowballs at their heads.
There were times we had snowball fights
With whosoever came into our sight.

It was a terrible shame and an awful disgrace
For someone with a snowball to wash your face.
I am older now, but I can still recall
How much fun I had throwing many snowballs.

HOW TO MAKE THE SICK, SICKER

When visiting the sick the thing to do,
Is to ask questions, "Do you have the flu?"
Say, "Don't let them give you too many pills,
You may get sicker and have a chill."

"Do not let them give you any blood,
It could be contaminated, and contain some mud."
"They said the person that had your bed, began
hemorrhaging in the head."

"They say the undertaker checks on you each day,
To see if you are alive or passed away."
"They say sick folks in here don't seem to last;
They're alive today; that night they pass."

"If I was you, I would pack up and leave,
And find some other place to retrieve;"
"Well it's time for me to get up and go;
I have warned you and told you so."

"All they want from you is money;
They don't care about your health honey."
"You just do the best you can,
And don't be operated on by just any old man."

"Find out what school he graduated from;
He may be a quack or just a bum.
All these doctors never went to school,
Some of them are mechanics handling tools."

"I'm going home and pray for you,
I don't know what good that will do,
These hospitals and nurses are a mess,
Only God can get you over this test."

"Goodbye, I love you!"

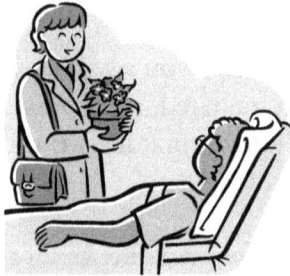

BEING A SENIOR CITIZEN IS INCONVENIENT

The worse season for a Senior Citizen is the fall.
That's when their hair falls out; their teeth fall out.
They fall up, they fall down, they fall out, and they

fall in the bed. They fall out of the bed; they fall out with what they see in the mirror. They even fall out with each other.

An officer walked up to a Senior Citizen and said, "I notice you've been standing here for sometime; can I be of any help?"

The Senior Citizen replied, "Yes, I put my shoes on the wrong foot, and I don't know what direction I want to go in."

The Senior Citizen went into a Chinese restaurant, and ordered a bowl of rice. Later he called the waiter. "I think I have a worm in my rice; it's moving."

The waiter answered, "We don't charge extra for meat for Senior Citizens on Wednesdays."

A Senior Citizen wanted to learn how to play the saxophone, so he asked the instructor, "How much will it cost?"

The Instructor answered, "We will have to charge you double."
The Senior Citizen asked, "Why is that?"
The Instructor replied, "It takes you too long to get your breath."

Senior Citizen: "Waiter, I see a fly on the top of my soup."
Waiter: "There's nothing to worry about. He's

practicing deep sea diving. He likes to show off."

MY DIFFERENT TWIN DAUGHTERS

I have two daughters and they are twins;
Not from outside appearances, but within.
Their behaviors are both the same,
Their heights are different and so are their names.

One is short the other one is tall;
When the two meet, they really have a ball.
The sound of their voices is just alike;
Each of their gestures is out of sight.

They are the real identical twins
Which first started from within;
If ever you are around them you will see,
How alike a pair twins can be.

WHOA

Because her car had tinted windows
Behind her she couldn't see.
If I had not hollered out
She would have backed over me.

THAT WAS SOME VISIT

One day my relatives came to visit me,
And decided to stay a little while.
When they came my house was very quiet,
But later on it became quite wild.

They looked into my refrigerator and saw my food
was low, so they decided to go shopping at the
nearby grocery store.

What they bought back I was completely amazed;
They said, "It should last us for at least a couple
days."

They said, "You may never know, the weather just
may change; It just might snow tomorrow and later
turn to rain."
Whoever heard of snow in the middle of July?
Was that the truth, or were they telling me a lie?

They stayed so long I packed up and moved out;
I think they were planning to stay forever;
In my mind there was no doubt.

So I called my landlord and told him what I had
done; He went and wrote them a lease; that night
they were on the run.

I peeked around the corner as they were tipping
out; I started jumping, and hollering and even let
out a shout.

51

Now I'm back into my house and I'm there to stay;
When relatives come to visit me, I tell them in a
nice way;

"There is a fine little hotel right down the street;
And they've got the loveliest people you ever want
to meet."

Now when they call me on my private telephone;
It will answer, "Sorry, no one here is at home."

THE LION AND THE SKUNK

There was a lion in the jungle who was not afraid of
any of the animals around him. One day he met a
skunk and began to express his power of how
powerful he was.

The skunk was explaining to the lion, the air around
him chases many of the animals away once they get
a whiff of this strong breeze.

The lion replied, "Nothing can chase me away,
breeze or no breeze." "Alright" said, the skunk. "I'll
be right back, I'm going to the washroom."
"Alright", said the lion, "Hurry back." The skunk
went into the brushes and came out. The skunk
hollered out,

"Lion, where are you?" A mile down the road the
lion roared back. "That's the strongest breeze I ever
breathed. I am running and crawling on my knees;
that's the first time, I ever smelled that breeze."

THE DOUBLE CROSS

The double cross is a hurtful word,
Used by a few not seldom heard.

When one placed trust into a friend,
And the outcomes are a bitter end.

For words one is entirely lost,
And tells the party, I been double crossed.

You tricked me, you fooled me, I thought you were
true. I thought you could be trusted;
I put my faith in you.

Confidence in you I now have lost;
I didn't think you would pull the double cross.

To be double crossed brings aches and pains;
The feelings and hurt cannot be explained.

I thought we were honest with each other;
I treated like you were my little kid brother.
To lose a good friend can be a terrible loss; not so
if you been double crossed.

THE ANIMALS ANNUAL PICNIC

The Ant, Antelope, and the Ape, were told to bring
some crumbs, cantaloupes, and grapes. The Badger,
Bat, and the Bear, was told to bring what they could
spare.

The Bees, Beetle, and the Birds must bring some
honey, worms and herbs. They told the Camel, the
Cat and the Cattle, bring some food and not your
rattles.

The greedy Cormorant who is so discreet was told
to bring something they all could eat. They told the
Crane, Cuckoo, the Deer and the Dog, don't bring
any food here you may get from the Hog.

The Donkey and the Dove, were told to bring
something they all loved. The Eagle, the Elephant,
and the Fish are to bring the salad dish.

They told the flea, the Fly the Fox and Frog; don't
bring anything you may find under the logs. The
Goat, the Grasshopper, and the Hare was warned
don't bring the same things as the Bear.

The Horse, the Leopard, the Lion and Lizard
prayed for sunshine, and no blizzard. The Mole, the
Moth, and Mouse started running when they saw
the Skunk and his spouse.

"Since you didn't invite me and my family; you can
go back to your holes and your trees.
So I'll see you around this time next year;
Hoping you all will be with me right here."

ANIMALS ANNUAL PICNIC CANCELLED

The Animals Annual Picnic cancelled.
Due to a sudden change in our environment
beyond our control, the Skunk stunk up the place;
darn his soul.

NICE STOOL WATER

"Get me some water baby." And she did.
I drank the water like a thirsty pig.

I said, "Baby that water was nice and cool,
Where did you get it from?"
She said, "Out of the toilet stool."

NO TIME FOR CONCEIT

After examinations, the Doctor said he needed rest;
she was the kind of woman who always wanted the
best.

Don't worry how the Doctor says you may feel;
Get back to work; you have a strong will.
Well he listened to her and did just that;
Shortly afterward, he was flat on his back.

The Doctor came out the room and said,
Your husband has just been pronounced dead.
He told you of his heart condition, but you were a
woman of strong ambition.

Now that you are on your own,
You must do your planning all alone.
So many eyes are not satisfied;

And so many desires are never complete.
These things happen in life because
One is full of vanity and conceit.

BABY SAM AND HIS FEATHER

I picked up a Bird feather off the ground
But its owner couldn't be found
I stopped and asked a nearby tree
If he knew where its owner could be?

He spoke up quietly and said
Asked the next tree up ahead
So I walked up to the next tree
And asked, "Do you know where its owner could be?"

He said with plenty of good luck
Go ask that flock of ducks
So I asked the ducks, "Who's in command?"
Then the tall one stood up and said, "I am."

I explained I found this feather on the ground
"Could you please tell me, where its owner can be found?"
He took the feather in his hands
Looked and said, "It belongs to Baby Sam."

I said, "Where does this Baby Sam live?
His feather to him I must give"
He said, "Walk down near the old oak tree
And you will see Baby Sam and his family."

As I ran fast and hurried on down
I heard crying all around
I asked, "Who's making that weeping sound?"
"My Baby lost his feather and cannot be found."

I took the feather out of my hand
The Mother shouted it belong to little Sam.
She got a needle and thread and began to sing;
As she sewed back Sam's lost wing.

Little Sam was happy and began to cry
Once again he said, "I can fly! I can fly!"
He and his friends flew up in the air
Flying up and down and everywhere.

Now when the birds get together
They all sing about
How Baby Sam found his feather.

MAYFIELD CARE CENTER

I returned to the place
Where my Mother once stayed.
I saw the receptionist, janitors,
And their maids.

They all greeted me with a happy smile, and said,"
We haven't seen you in quite a while."

Since my Mother doesn't reside there any more,
There is no need for me to enter those doors.
But I came back with a word to say,
How nice they treated my Mother
From day to day.

Some things you may find and
Very hard to replace.
Are the wonderful people here
And it shows in their faces.

HANDSOME DON JUAN

Handsome Don Juan, was called the women's gift
Sweet names by them he was called
He was young, danced and also fancy
He really thought he had it all.

With beautiful girls around his arms
He would put on his best of charms
Now that Don Juan is now up in age
No more over him do the women rage.

In the mirror he now sees
He's not the Don Juan he used to be
In the mirror he looks and stares
Wondering, what have happened to his hair?

His mouth gets a great relief
At night when he takes out his teeth
And every time when it begins to rain
His body aches with stiffness and pains.

Those golden days for him have passed
But his memories will always last
All the girls can now see
Old Don Juan isn't what he used to be.

I THOUGHT WRONG

I thought in order to have fun
You had to have women and a bottle of
rum.

A car about two blocks long
And plenty of money to show yourself strong.

You must have a wardrobe with nice clothes
Dressed to kill from head to toe.

It's a must to have these things
Gold, silver and diamond rings.

Two or three women at your side
For your pleasure to satisfy.

WILBURN CARLOS

There was a fella who was a gigolo
He took sick and went down slow.

He had tons of fun and lots of thrills
He got sick and couldn't pay his bills

He carried his belongings to the pawn shop
His suits, rings and even his socks.

All of his friends he used to know
Learned he was broke and let him go.

One day to the hospital he went
Broke, busted and not a red cent
Then a few days later, they pronounced dead

As I looked down on his body
I remember a song
I thought this was living
But I was dead wrong

This is a story with a very sad end
He had no church, family or friends

His burial will not take place
Until money is raised to buy him space

I thought in order to have your fun
You had to have women, cars and some rum
If these things one often craves
He is sure to have an untimely grave.

TWO GUIDES

There are two spirits in our world
Each day they are in a fight
One takes a stand for wrong
The other takes a stand for right.

One begs and says, "Follow me
And I will supply all of your needs."
The other spirit gives convincing advice
Which sounds good, but won't suffice.

He will promise you riches, silver, and gold
In exchange for your very soul
He will lead you down a one way route
Knowing for you there's no way out.

Many that was headed right
Turned the good voice aside
Later they felt so ashamed
They sought a place to hide.

Two spirits with a different voice
It's up to you, you have a choice.

TIME

I sat on my bed watching the clock
It kept on ticking and wouldn't stop
So I decided to move back time
And turned back the hands to fit my mind.

I don't know what I was thinking about
Time is something you cannot shut out
Time moves on and it is true
Time doesn't wait for me or you.

PLANT ENOUGH

I planted a garden one beautiful day
The thieves came and stole it away
"I asked myself what must I do?"
The thought came, plant enough for two

Now when the thieves come to steal
I really, really don't care
They don't know what they are doing
Is only stealing their share.

THE DAD THEY NEVER KNEW

They said, he was my father
At least that's what I was told
How could he be my father
A man that's grey and old?

Other kids' fathers I did know
They were around to watch them grow
In the woods they would take a hike
Played together, rode a bike.

Even at school at graduations times
There they saw their father
Standing in line.

When they were just little boys
Their lives were filled with happiness and joy
When Sunday mornings rolled around
Together in churches they were found.

Now their dad has grown old
They still remember the stories they were told
In many homes it was true they had a father
Someone they never knew.

Oh the fun they could have had
If only they knew the man called Dad.

IT'S BEST TO PLAN FIRST

If you failed to build on a solid rock
You may be in for a terrible shock
You could face storms, also floods
Not to mention tornadoes and mud.

So take your time to make your plans
If these things come, you mostly likely will stand
Because you considered and did stock;
A foundation of strong solid rocks.

BLESSING IN DISGUISE

To lose your money is bad
To lose your health is worse
To lose a nagging spendthrift wife
Is heaven to one on earth.

DANG

On the ground I found a twenty dollar bill,
When I stoop to pick up,
I realized it wasn't really real.

FORGOTTEN CANDLES ON THE MANTLE

An old candle box laid on the shelf
Had been there for a period of time
All by themselves.

Old burned out stems were very low
Useless it seemed time for them to go
When they were bought they were brand new;
Now there's nothing more for them to do.

There were strange people in the nursing home;
Some received visitors. Some had none.
It would be nice if we decided to bake
For all of them a welcome cake.

The cake was taken there for a treat
Now they all can enjoy something to eat

"Something is missing," someone said,
What could it be as we scratched our heads?

Then I remembered with a smile so bright
The cake is dark and needed some light
They took the candles off the shelf
Each stood alone all by themselves.

What a wonderful time it was for all
Watching each candle stand proud and tall;
Although long forgotten and set aside
When lit that evening they burned with pride.

BRING YOUR OWN RULES

Basketball, football, we played them all,
Sometimes there were arguments.
Sometimes there was a brawl.

Our games were never complete,
Because one team had to cheat.

That was our way of letting off steam,
And felt good if you were the winning team.

And when we played cards in the dark,
There was always pool and card sharks.

Sometimes all the back of the cards were red;
And when some were blue, you would scratch your
head.

That was the way our games were played; we
brought our own rules and nothing was said.

As you counted your winnings walking down the
streets; you wouldn't have won if you didn't cheat.

MY SNAKE VILLA

In the morning on my grass,
My snakes wave at me when they pass.
After having a good night sleep,
They crawl away searching for food to eat.

If you see my snakes leave them alone,
They all live here in this their home.
All of my snakes are happy and free,
And we all enjoy each other's company.

PITCHING PENNIES

Pitching pennies to the line,
Was a game we played often to pass time.
The nearest penny to the line would win; and
whoever did would laugh and grin.

Each player had a certain way,
To make their penny do as they say.
At least that what they had in mind,
Seemed sometimes it worked, not all the time.

There was old penny pitching Pete,
Who was always looking for a way to cheat.

His feet was never in its place, and he would put
gum on his penny face.

If your penny would bounce and roll,
That meant you had no control.
When two pennies looked like a tie,
There was measuring, arguments, and lot of lies.

Pitching pennies is a lot of fun,
Not if you lose, only if you won.
It was a way of passing time,
To see if your skill was better than mine.

WHEN PAPA LOST HIS JOB

Around the table we would gather to eat, with
delicious cakes, pies, and all sort of treats.
Our house was full of laughter and lots of fun,
there were happy faces on every one.

We had no worries or any cares,
We had plenty and often shared.
We would go picnicking in the parks,
And arrive home before the dark.

We were happy and full of joy,
A bunch of girls and also boys.
One day Papa came home with a strange look, and
we heard him tell Ma his job they took.

They told him to pack his things and go,
They wouldn't need him there anymore.
Ma was quiet not a word she said,

As Papa walked away with a bow down head.

As children we didn't know what it was all about,
and was soon told we would have to move out.
The serving on our plate was sometimes small;
there was times we hardly ate at all.

Sometimes we would heard Papa pray,
Hoping things will get better for us all someday.
We were shocked and greatly surprised,
When we saw tears coming from Papa eyes.

On a truck we packed our toys and clothes;
I carried my doll with her shiny nose.
In a far away corner I could hear Ma sob;
Because it was a sad day when Papa lost his job.

WHERE IS TRUTH?

In court he raised his hand to tell the truth; soon
lies began dropping from his tooth.

Do you swear before the almighty God?
It's a wonder he wasn't struck by a lightning rod.

To tell the truth has become a thing of the past;
telling lies now are seated in first class.

Folk will look you dead in the eye.
And say if I'm lying I hope to die.

To take an oath don't mean a thang,
To some it's like playing a game.

So be conscious, right and tell the truth,
Or tell a lie and feel free and loose.

WHAT HAS HAPPENED?

People had a conscious a long time ago,
What's happening to them today I don't know.
My conscious told me to come and apologize;
I was wrong I realize.

Last night I could not sleep,
I owe you money and I want it to keep.

My conscious said, "Come and pay you back; be
honest and stay on the right track."

Hey Man, what did your conscious say?
It left me; I think it ran away.

When we were together in the bed the other day,
He said, "I don't want to hear what you have to
say."

"You owe folks thousands of dollars,
The same ones that gave you their shirts and
collars."

"Your best friend saw you coming down the
streets; he hasn't seen you in a month and two
weeks."

"The finance company said for you to call; or they
are coming in a truck to make a haul."

Folks leave messages on your phone,
The answering service says, "I'm not at home."

People seem to swindle you or forget to pay;
Will see you coming and go the other way.

Society has now left all morals behind.
This you will learn, not in the nick of time.

WHAT A SURPRISE!

What a surprise! What a surprise! What a surprise!
When he looked up into the Judge's eyes.

He was involved in a car accident,
The other car fender he had bent.

He came out of his car in a rage,
Had no respect for the other driver's age.

If the police had not been around,
He probably would have beaten the man to the
ground.

He was told come to court present your case,
Tell your side to the Judge's face.

"Court now in session, please stand,
The honorable Judge is now on hand."

"Case number #40 take the stand now,"
The defendant looked up and hollered, "Wow!"

Suddenly he fainted and fell down;
No smelling salt could bring him around.

They bumped him and pumped him,
As he opened up his eyes;
He said, "Forget it, I'm not facing that guy."

THE END OF THE LOVER'S SPAT

"You are not going to walkout on me," she said.
"Before you do, I'll see you dead.

Funeral arraignments are now pending,
The lover's spat came to an ending.

If he had only used his head,
He would still be living instead of dead.

Listen to what your lover might say
And don't just get up and walk away.

Smooth her gently whenever you can,
And let her know you are her man.

SLOW DOWN

I bit into an apple that was red
When a worm hollered out,
"Don't bite my head."

But the poor worm hollered too late;
If he was on the other side
He would have escaped.

SONNY DILLARD THE CAMOUFLAGED LIZARD

Sonny Dillard was truly a lizard,
You could name the tricks he would do
To any person that came along
No matter where or who.

On the corner having a ball,
The cops came by and made a haul.
They took to the station not one, but all.

Sonny and Martin were together in a cell
When suddenly out broke hell.
Water was poured into Martin's shoe,
And he asked Sonny," What did you do?

Sonny said, "I saw the guard making a creep,
And put water in your shoes while you were sleep."
"I noticed in his hand he had a cup,
And I didn't feel like waking you up."

Martin said, "Are you trying to make a fool out of me?"
Sonny replied, "He's the only one that's got a key."
Back and forth they would argue and fuss;
At each other they would holler and cuss.

In the jail some of us had fun; not so for everyone.
Martin left feeling sad and blue, because he knew
Sonny put water in his shoe;
After all, in the cell were just those two.

NO EXCEPTIONS

Once a story to me was told,
How you get less attention
When you grow old.

You can't keep up, you can't move fast.
You soon become part of the forgotten class.

Your friends and your children just may say, "All
you ever do is sit all day."

You can look back and remember when; they
carried you places now and then.

There were times they came to your door; saying
"Let's go visiting, let's explore."

Now you sit alone and to yourself sing
No knocks on the doors; no telephone rings.

These things happen sometimes in life,
If you were once a husband or once a wife.

Loved ones you once held so dear,
Now they are gone, seemed to have disappeared.

No matter if it's age, confinement, or handicapped
Things happen to them all, and that's a fact.

So look over your shoulders back in the past;
And remember your good old days,
And how long they last.

There's no need to be sad or blue,
Somewhere, someone is thinking about you.

Though you sit by yourself in your home; there is
an unseen guest,
Who will never leave you alone.

LET ME LIVE TOO

While sitting in the window sill
Catching the sunshine over me as it spills.
And its warm breath I can feel,
As my roots in me stand still.

I am only a plant in the house
With its leaves of dazzling green.
When I'm watered and cared for
My beauty can all be seen.

People notice and admire me too
How I once was small and how I grew.
If where I am and gathering dust
Just wipe me gentle, please don't fuss.

Don't place me out in the shade
Where my leaves may dry and also fade.
Be good to me and also kind
And I'll be with you for a long, long, time.

I SAW HER

There on the corner holding a cup,
Hoping some change she may pick up.
I gave some quarters, nickels, and dimes;
Something I enjoy doing most of the time.

We may never know when we may join,
Others on the streets seeking some coins.
Life can carry you down and also up,
Who knows, one day we may be holding a cup.

DON'T THROW IN THE TOWEL

Throw in the towel is a form of speech,
When the end we think we have reached.
We may say, "I'm giving up, what's the use?"
Then for some reason we make an excuse.

Hold back your towels a little bit longer,
What strength you have will get stronger.
If you've got faith some way somehow,
Dig in deep and begin to plow.

Many that thought they were behind,
Moved up swiftly to the front of the line.
So get a strong grip and wear a big smile,
And tell yourself, we're not throwing in the towel.

WILL BE BACK SOON

He was never so embarrassed as before,
To see his wife lying naked on the floor.
What's going on; why is she down there
Where are her clothes; why is she bare?

She and her friends were having a toast,
She happened to take an overdose.
Leave her alone, leave her be
She is not able to recognize you or me.

Her thoughts and mind are no longer there,
Her spirit is now traveling far into the air.
She is now visiting her secret outer space,
Where strange things in her will take place.

Hallucinations will guide her condition,
It will control her soul and her position.
She will go to many planets and maybe the moon,
When will she return? I cannot say how soon.

BRING ME

Bring to me your tears drops,
And I'll turn them into gold.
And make each one sparkle,
Like diamonds standing in a row.

SLICK FOLKS

Some folks wear the title called slick
They are very cunning and full of tricks.

They can look you dead in the eye
And yet tell you unbelievable, unheard lies.

If they can capture your attention and your mind
With their talk that sound so fine.

Then they will tell you about some gain
That will bring you fortune and fame.

These are scam artists and known as pros; using the
same old stories wherever they go.

To them it's a game and lots of fun
After they trick you they're on the run.

Though time, days and hours may pass
Their trickery can't always last.

What is it slick folks do not know?
One day they will reap what they sow.

WE KISSED ON THE BRIDGE

On the bridge together we kissed,
Lips so tender who could resist.
As the cars drove swiftly by
We saw only kisses in each other's eyes.

As the waters flowed underneath
A view of us they sought to seek.
When the birds flew over our heads,
They too wanted to hear what was being said.

As both of our lips touched each others,
Not one sound did we utter.
On the bridge together we kissed,
Lips warm and tender, how could I resist?

TRUE

There are some things
Some folks don't need to know.
They will tell it wrong
Where ever they may go.

Just as sure as they are born
They will get the horse by his horns.
They will turn a mole hill
Into a mountain.
And swear they saw
A frozen watery fountain.

Here is a very helpful clue
And the right thing for one to do
Keep your thoughts inside of you.
Only you will know what's true.

CAGE FREE

I put my little bird into her cage
Asked her to sing me a song
She opened her mouth and said,
This isn't where I belong.

So I opened up her cage
And she flew up in a tree
Now she sings day and night
Since she is now free.

SOME PEOPLE I MET AND CAN NEVER FORGET.

OLD BEN

Old Ben was as big as an ox
Would eat anything from a plate or box.
A pot of greens or a pot of beans
They would quickly disappear off the scene.

All the folks in the neighborhood knew old Ben
He was big and kind; a very good friend.
He would work free and without pay
As long as a plate of food came his way.

He was mannerable, gracious, full of thanks;
Would appreciate even pork-n-beans and franks.
Making him a large pitcher of lemonade
Or a cup of cold water or some nice cool ade.

Well, Ben's family moved from the old
neighborhood;
His whereabouts were never known.
But we know where ever there was food
Ben would make himself at home.

SOMEONE WE MET AND CAN NEVER FORGET.

LOUISE OR PUNK

She was named Louise, but we called her punk,
She could dance and that was no bunk.

It didn't matter if you were short or tall; she would
dance smoothly with them all.

She would dance with grace and stride
While couples watched her on the side.
Her name was Louise but they called her punk,
She was a good dancer and that was no bunk.

SMART

The early bird catches the worms,
So all the worms got smart.
Instead of getting up real early
They now get a late, late, start.

CHANGING THE RULES

How can you change the rules
In the middle of a game
Are you crazy, have you gone insane ?

I am the official that sits at the top
I decide what goes and what goes not.
If things aren't going my way
Then I change the rules right away.

I know what rules are in the books
They are for honest people, not for crooks
The rules are for loyal folks
To find that kind is just a joke.

Everyone, at one time or another
Brings in new rules they've just discovered
And the rules they bring about
Is an escape to help them out.

Changing the rules is nothing new
It's done by many, not just a few.
Everywhere the rules are the same
To change the rules, some act insane.

Back them in a corner and they will say
They just changed the rules the other day;
In your mind let this thought remain
They can change the rules in any game.

NOT AGAIN

I met a woman and it's sad to say
Each time I saw her, it was her birthday.

So I got wise to her old tricks
And told her I was broke, and just been sick.

When she would walk down the streets
Saying, "This is my birthday" to all she would meet.
"Congratulations" they all would say,
None stopped, but kept on their way.

SMEAR CAMPAIGN

The tactic of a smear campaign is to take an
opponent and destroy his name.
Go to his home town and find out who
Remember what he did at the age of two.

His mother and father, what were they like? Are
they together, do they quarrel, drink and fight?

They will dig down deep into your past
Until they come up with something at last.

A smear campaign can really, really, hurt; after
others keep digging, looking for dirt.

And what some diggers do not know
They are no better than the guy next door.

WHATEVER HAPPENED TO LITTLE RICHARD?

Whatever happen to little Richard
To tell the truth, I don't know.
The last I'd seen and heard of him,
Was a very long time ago.

His mother was very beautiful,
Beautiful as she could be.
But little Richard she neglected,
By his appearance that you could see.

The crowd she would gather around
And the company she would keep
Loved to party and loved to drink,
And never had time to sleep.

His friends would poke fun at him,
And ask, "Where's your drinking mother?"
Little Richard would drop his head,
And not a word he would mutter.

A prominent person was standing by
When he got Richard's attention and replied,
"Let me adopt you and make you my son;"
And for Richard immediately this was done.

From his surroundings he was taken away;
While his mother continued to drink day by day.
Once he said, "Ma, let's go home,"
But she preferred to be left alone.

Soon afterward his mother passed away
And his new home there he stayed.
Whatever happen to little Richard it was told;
He's now happy and sparkles like gold.

WHATEVER HAPPENED TO LEN?

Whatever happened to Len?
He gets out of jail and goes back again.
It may be difficult for one to say
What could have happened to him one day.

In this life we don't why, the reasons some folks
laugh and other folks may cry.
Some folks conquer life's strong brinks. While
others may slow down and attend to strong drinks.

It may be hard to say why some people go astray.
Heavy problems they may face
And decide to leave life's swift race.

When we asked them to explain, why throw away
what they have gained?
Their answer to you just may be to understand you
must be me.

Inside could be a hidden need,
Why some fail to succeed.
To understand their point of view,
You must be them and not be you.

ONE LESS

Around the dinner table they would pile
Full of laughter full of smiles.
Food cooking at its best,
Not the same with one less.

You could smell the aroma in the air,
Cakes and pies seemed everywhere.
After dinner what a mess,
Things not the same with one less.

Fond memories in each other's mind,
And the joy they had one time.
Now mom lays at rest, family not the same, with
one less.

Tasty foods are now all gone,
All are grown now on their own.
Remembered how all one time was blessed; life is
not the same now with one less.

WHEREVER YOU ARE MY LOVE

Wherever you are my love, I will find you,
In some café my love, or some rendezvous.
I will walk a million miles, you will know by my
smiles,
And wherever you are my love, I will find you.

In my dreams my love there were we two,
Beneath the skies my love of starlight blue,

In my arms we hugged and kissed,
When I woke you were a mist;
And wherever you are my love, I will find you.

Wherever you are my love, I will find you,
Wherever you are my love, no one else will do.

And I promise you that I will find you before I die,
And wherever you are my love, and wherever you
are my love,
And wherever you are my love I will find you.

DO YOU WANT TO TRADE WITH ME?

Would you like to trade places with me?
Give me your eyes that I may see?

Everything you see, you see something wrong
Why are you so hard to get along?

You never seem to be satisfied
Just what do you see through your eyes?

I see the little birdies in the air
I see the sun shining so bright and fair.

With my sensitive and precious nose
I see flowers wearing clothes.

You need to trade places me
So you can see the things I see.

ELLINGTON AND HIS FRIEND LEAH

Ellington and Leah are a pair
They can be seen together everywhere
In the house or on the streets
These two you will always meet

Down the block together they run
With laughter and having much fun
Ellington is so fast and strong
Sometimes he drags Leah along

Ellington guardian we call Kim
Cannot do too much with him
He's now in Leah hand
And do what she commands

Kim looks at Ellington and wonders why; he
sometimes passes her by.
The secret to all of this; Leah has affection,
Ellington cannot resist.

ONCE WHEN

Once when couples walked down the aisles; they
were very sincere in their vows. It was said, until
death do we part
Those words no longer are found in one's heart.

It started out for better or worse
Nowadays, they sound like a curse
The once sweet couple of man and wife
Instead of love, there's bitterness and strife.

There was laughter and gaiety at the wedding;
happiness forever they both said.
Great fun they had together;
Memories of a happy couple couldn't get any
better.

Now that their journey has come to an end
Though they are separated,
They can still be friends.

Here comes the bride, but where is the groom?
Someone said, "He left the room."

A SUPER DUPER SALES PERSON

I went into a shopping store to spend less money,
not much more.
For my shoes I bought shoe strings
The sales person sold me other things.

He looked down at my feet; said, "New shoes on
you will look neat." New shoes weren't on my list;
he showed me a suit; I couldn't resist.

This new suit said the clerk
Will look good with a brand new shirt
So this lovely shirt I did buy
He went and picked out a beautiful tie.

He put my things in a box;
And happened to notice a hole in my socks.
I hurried and got out of there;
After I brought a hat, pajamas and underwear.

If you meet a sales person who is a fast talker;
Turn around and be a walker.
If I had stayed inside that door,
He would have sold me the entire store.

THE REPO MAN

The finance company sent me a letter
Stating I was behind in my bills
That I already knew
They should have asked, "How do I feel?"

If I'm behind in my payments
To me that's no big deal
They will get their money for sure
They know that I'm for real.

I first have a little catching up to do
You see I lost some money at the track
I spent a few dollars more than expected
Trying to win some of it back.

I had scheduled for me vacation trips
On one of those fine luxury ships
The company knew I loved to entertain
And I love to play the money game.

There's no need for them to worry
I'll pay them soon; there's no hurry
They send me letters all the time
It's a wonder I don't lose my mind.

"Honey, where did you park the car?
I parked it in front of the door"
"That's funny, it's not here anymore."

"Pick up the phone call the police,
My car was stolen by some thieves."

They said, "A man came by in a truck"
They saw him stop and pick it up.

"Did they stop to get his name?"
"He said his name was Repo,"
Re-pos-ses –sion was his game.

I went to the office to pick up my check
They said, "Repo came first."
My day was a wreck.

I went back to my beautiful house
Outside was my furniture and my spouse.

I asked, "Honey what are you doing out here?"
She said, "Repo came by early, my dear."
"They took our fridge, stove and our chairs
Even the comb while straitening my hair."

"They even took our brand new television;
To stop payments was your decision."

Remember this and it's a fact
If you find your payments getting slack
To pay your bills and you forget
Repo will come when you least expect.

MA, DON'T WAIT UP FOR ME

Ma, the other day I got some mail
On a ship I must sail
I'll be going to a strange country
So Ma, please don't wait up for me.

There's a war now in the land
And they are calling for a dedicated man.
Tomorrow we are headed out to sea;
So Ma, please don't wait up for me.

We have now landed on the ground
All is peaceful, not a sound
If there's danger none can see
So Ma, please don't wait up for me.

When I was just a little child
And would travel miles and miles
A bright light I would see
And there you were waiting up for me

Now your only son is at war
And thousands more like he
Cannons, noises all around
So Ma, please don't wait up for me

We have dug deep into our holes
The weather here is very cold
We are surrounded by our enemies
So Ma, please don't wait up for me.

MR. RIGHT

Mr. Right lived all alone
Set out to find Miss Right for his home.
Other women he had met
Only to chit and sometimes chat.

Well, one day Miss Wright came along
She was always right and never wrong.
How would these two get along?
Like beautiful music to a song.

The first two weeks they did just fine,
After two weeks what's yours is mine.
And to be sure of no mistakes
Please don't upset me for heaven's sake.

"But Darling, you appeared to be so kind;"
"I still am, are you out of your mind?"
But you said, the most sweetest things
When on your finger I placed that ring.

We were like two fishes caught in a net
What was said then, Babe you can now forget.

We are together and will be for life
You are my husband and I am your wife.
Just do as I say, there won't be no strife.

I have six sisters and five brothers
Sometime I had to act like I was the mother.
I have experience and practice too,
So don't you come telling me what to do.

Sometimes we would argue and sometimes fight;
about who was wrong and who was right.
But you and I won't have no regrets
Because I was all Wright before we met.

And to your friends don't try to explain
About taking that W out of my name.
I am now your Mrs. Right.

I cannot be wrong, but have always been Wright.
Just because some words sound just alike;
You better make sure and get your spelling right.

NOT ANY MORE

Many, many, years ago marriage was fine
Now if you got married today.
You are completely out of your mind.

You can't tell me what to do
I'm not a child, I'm grown.
I have always been that way
Ever since I left home.

Don't tell me what to do
I got a job just like you.
If I come in that door late
Don't wait for me, fix your own plate.

If you loved how your mom cooked,
You never should have gotten yourself hooked.

Go get that bottle off the shelf
I didn't have this baby by myself.

I know darn well I don't look the same
How can I with this fat I have gained?
It's too bad if your feelings are hurt
Had we both known, we coulda remained in
church.

We even said, for better or worse, even to death
Let's go over our vows, and see what's left.
If you are tired, please let me know
Get used to it honey, there's no place to go.

They said years ago marriage was fine
People then had a made up mind.
Honey let's do the best we can
Since I'm your woman, and you are my man.

COURT SCENE

Judge, "Your wife seems sweet, lovely, and kind."
Husband, "Your Honor you give me your wife and
you take mine."

What goes on behind our closed door.
Are words spoken you never heard before.

In her church you should hear her sing,
She was an old devil wearing artificial wings.

I come home hungry want to know what she
cooked; she put her hands on her hips and gives me
a dirty look.

Her Pastor said, "Would you like to renew your
vow?" Deep down inside of me you can hear me
growl.

If I could take her back to the altar again,
I would be guilty of the runaway sin.
When she sings, "Some glad morning I'll fly away;
Lord knows I can't wait for that day."

When the Pastor said, "For better or worse;"
I knew I was in trouble when we drove off in a
hearse.

When a Preacher tells you to say I do,
You'd better take your time and think it through.
And if she says I don't have all day,
Look for the nearest exit and make your getaway.

HIS LAST DANCE WITH ME

He came to me, and asked if I would dance; I
looked him over, and decided to take a chance.
When we had reached the crowded large floor;
His swinging me around soon made me sore.

When he spun me around his neck
I thought I was coming out of a wreck.
So many times he turned me around
I felt like I was dancing upside down.

As my blue dress flew in the air
People, looked, laughed and stared,
I said, "If this music don't hurry up and stop;
On this floor I am going to drop."

Well, the music and the dance came to an end;
I hurried on back to my friends.
Oh how they did laugh and scream;
And said I was a sight to be seen.

I went and sat down to get some rest
Trying hard to catch my breath
The music started up once again
And here comes this unacquainted friend.

He asked me to dance with him just once more; I
told him my body was very sore. He said,
"Together, I think we dance well; I'm quite sure
you can tell."

He said he had never danced before
With any girls on a dance floor
Only me and heaven knows how many times he
stepped on my toes.

I was very polite, in trying to explain
My poor body wasn't feeling the same.
He smiled, turned, and walked away
Under my breath I whispered,
"This is your last time José."

PLEASURE IN DEATH

Don't you dare when I am dead
Come weeping and crying over my head;
For the things you failed to do,
And murmuring tears you have been untrue.

Since I am alive, you wish I would go'
Somewhere even you don't know.
So don't you dare weep over my head,
When I'm stretched out and looking dead.

I got a job and worked for you;
But you felt like I should have had two.
I worked my fingers to the bone;
And that's what I would eat when I got home.

Not only does my insurance cover
Your entire family, including your mother.
But your expenses for twenty years;
So there's nothing honey for you to fear.

All I ask is just one thing;
Promise me that you will sing.
Not a song you may suggest;
But one that will let me rest.

So when I placed below the ground;
Where all is quiet and not a sound.
Let not those tears flood your cheeks;
And find you acting humble and meek.

For the things you failed to do;
And worried me until I was blue.
Now I'm alive, you wish I were dead;
And when death does come, don't water my head.

PEE WEE AND HIS WHISTLING

Pee Wee could whistle very loud,
His whistling stood above the crowd.
On the streets, or even at play,
You could hear him whistle every day.

One night some boys decided to steal some pies,
and Pee Wee was invited to be their spy.
If someone would come along, he would whistle
them a warning song.

They stole some pies and all went well,
Some they ate, and some they would sell.
Then one warm summer night,
His friend decided to steal a bike.

He brought Pee Wee along,
Just to whistle a warning song.
Well, his friend stole the bike
While Pee Wee whistled through the night.

The next morning while checking out the bike; the
one that was stolen that fateful night.
Pee Wee began to whistle a song,
When down the alley a family came along...

ABOUT THE AUTHOR

The roaring twenties roared a little bit louder when Wilburn "Pee Wee" Carlos entered the earth. Born in 1921, Wilburn roared with the twenties, became culturally enlightened during the Harlem Renaissance, and along with most of America, tightened his belt during the Great Depression.

In the 1930s, swing was king, and so was Daddy. An aspiring drummer with the Count Basie band, there wasn't an instrumentalist, jazz composer, or band he didn't know about. Wilburn built a thriving shoe-shine business on California and Lake Street on Chicago's west side.

One other nickname Daddy had was Edo in high school. That was a name in Japanese history of economic growth, peace, and a thriving arts culture. Daddy developed a unique sense of style even back then, and maintained it throughout his life.

I believe he began writing poetry extensively in the late 1950s and early 1960s. He could literally write a poem at the drop of a hat. He viewed life from a different lens, as evidenced in his writings. I sincerely hope you have enjoyed this collection.

P.S. I would like you to complete daddy's poem, "*Pee Wee and His Whistling.*" He did get caught, because the woman of the child whose bike was stolen recognized his whistle. Let me know what you come up with.

Remember,
"Don't fall out with the cook; and if you fall, don't fall too far."

Photo taken December 16, 2011, shortly after celebrating his 90th birthday. He made his transition the very next day.

Other books by Wilburn Carlos:

Good Thoughts to Think On

Books by Kimberly F. Carlos:

Achieving Fulfillment in Education: A Lifeline in Challenging Times

Changing the Game to Fulfillment

Contact Information:
www.missdoctoratedu.com
866.949.8824
missdoctor4u@gmail.com

www.ingramcontent.com/pod-product-compliance
Lightning Source LLC
Chambersburg PA
CBHW031520040426

42445CB00009B/326